Harry Thomas Cory

Multiphase Alternating Current Transmission

Harry Thomas Cory

Multiphase Alternating Current Transmission

ISBN/EAN: 9783337192433

Printed in Europe, USA, Canada, Australia, Japan

Cover: Foto ©ninafisch / pixelio.de

More available books at **www.hansebooks.com**

Multiphase Alternating Current Transmission.

Thesis submitted
for the degree of
Master of Mechanical
Engineering in
Electrical Engineering
to the Faculty of Cornell University
June 1896.

The transmission of power by multiphase alternating currents is an outcome of the strenuous efforts of late years made for the purpose of rendering inaccessible sources of power accessible. In other words the attempt has been made to surpass Mohammed's great feat of bringing the Mountains to him, by another feat of greater difficulty, owing to the intangibility of the necessary components of it. How well this has been carried out the amazing growth and multiplication of power distribution plants will amply testify. Especially is meant those installations which derive their power from remote sources where great quantities of energy were previously being wasted in waterfalls and rivers.

The necessity for transmission is quite apparent when we consider the fact that manufacturing centers cannot always be placed away off in the mountains.

The necessity being realized the question becomes how to obviate it. And in this case it has been found that the only way in which power can be efficiently transmitted through long distances is by means of electricity. And at the present time the most satisfactory method which has yet presented itself is that of transmission by alternating currents differing in phase.

The economic transmission of power by electricity demands primarily high potential, both to save expense in copper and also at the same time to prevent excessive loss in heating effect due to the large currents which become

necessary with the use of low potential.

Since the power in watts of a current of electricity depends upon two factors, current and electro-motive force multiplied together, it follows that any given power may be obtained with widely varying values of the two factors pro[illegible]ing their product is constant. Thus 1000 watts may be transmitted by a current of 1000 amperes at a pressure of 1 volt,or by a current of 1 ampere at 1000 volts, or by 500 amperes at 2 volts and so on ad infinitum, providing that the product E C equals always 1000. Since the size of a conductor depends upon the magnitude of the current flowing through it, it is clear that to save copper the current must be small and the pressure correspondingly high. Furthermore, since the loss by heating varies as the square of the current another important reason for the use of small currents, that is high potentials, is evident. Thus we see the necessity for high tension transmission depends upon important commercial considerations.

It becomes necessary in order to prevent great first cost and to do away with excessive losses in operation.

Having established the important fact that high voltages are absolutely necessary, the reason for the use of alternating currents instead of direct currents will bear explanation.

The reason in question is not so much a commercial one as a practical one. The main consideration upon wheih the use of alternating currents depends is that of the wonderful flexibility of its applications. For instance,

if we have an alternator by the use of transformers containing no moving parts whatever it is possible to use the output of the generator at any potential whatever. And if the machine is a two or three phase one it is possible, and moreover practicable, to take from it currents of three or two phase no matter what the original current may have been. All of these transformations may be accomplished with small losses.

The importance of being able to obtain a high voltage from a low voltage machine is at once evident when we consider that the cost of transmission is lessened at high pressures, the cost of copper varying inversely as the square of the voltage, and moreover that it is practically impossible to build a dynamo that will stand high enough pressure to enable its output to be transmitted through great distances. It has been found that it is practically impossible to insulate the moving parts of generators giving an output at a potential of more than 3500 volts and current greater than 30 to 50 amperes. This pressure is bad enough t o deal with in an alternator where the moving contacts are extremely simple; but when it comes to the construction of a commutator to withstand this potential the problem becomes impossible when the current is large. The current simply jumps from bar to bar all around that commutator forming an arc around it, with the result that that important part is soon ruined.

Even suppose that it were possible to build direct current generators of high voltage, say 10000 for example,

it would still be impossible to run lights upon this current, and the apparatus for reducing this potential down to one not above the capacity of an incandescent lamp would involve the use of rotating parts requiring considerable attention and subject to continual wear. At the same time the efficiency of such rotary converters is not equal to that of transformers.

Of course if all the light and power to be supplied were situated immediately about the distribution center at the end of the line only one rotary converter would be needed. But in case the consumers were scattered over a considerable area the economical distribution of light and power would demand high potentials, so high in fact as to be prohibitive of the use of incandescent lamps without the use of the apparatus just mentioned. Even then every consumer cannot afford to have such an expensive and troublesome thing in his house as a rotary transformer, rotary con verter, motor-generator, motor-dynamo or dynamotor as it is variously called.

However this disagreeable necessity will be spared him for a while yet, since up to the present time no direct current dynamos have been constructed to run on so high a voltage of any great power.

Briefly, the superiority of the alternating current for transmission of light and power depends upon the readiness with which we can transform it up or down to any potential whatever by means of inert apparatus which can be insulated to withstand any pressure desired. This instru-

ment , the transformer, moreover, suffers no loss from wear and therefore requires absolutely no attention whatever. It can be put out in the rain on a pole and be left there for years without undergoing repair.

An alternating current power transmission plant would in its chief essentials consist of the following parts. First, at the source of power, say a waterfall, there would be an installation consisting of turbines or impact wheels running one or more alternators wound for a moderate difference of potential at the terminals. The current thus generated would be converted to one of high potential by means of step up transformers, and then transmitted to the distant point where it is to be utilized, converted to a current of sufficiently low potrntial by means of step down transformers, in order to render it applicable for use in lights or motors.

Until within the last few years it was impossible to follow out the above scheme with any economy on account of the inefficiency of alternating current motors. In fact it has only been comparatively recently that they have had any self starting alternating current motors at all that would run successfully. But at the present time the theory of alternating currents is much better understood, so that now motors are made to run on them with just as good results as obtained by the use of direct current motors. Still the use of alternating current motors is practically a new thing, but from what we have seen of them already it has been made evident that their use for the transmission

of power through long distances is far more efficient and is attended with far better results than have ever been realized by any other means.

In transmission work we have the choice of various systems, single phase, two phase and three phase. As is well known, the simple alternating current is of a pulsating character, the direction and intensity of the current varying regularily according to a well determined law. So that when we have a conductor moving in a magnetic field on the periphery of an armature the fluctuations of current and electro-motive force may be plotted in the form of a curve. The curve in many cases is sinusoidal.

In a polyphase current generator we have a machine which gives off several currents which pass through their zero values and attain their maxima at different times but still at regular intervals.

In a three phase dynamo for instance, we have an armature with three windings each giving a current differing 120 degrees in phase from the other. It is evident that in an ordinary alternating current the power at times is zero, it being also of a pulsating character. But in a polyphase current the power is practically constant, as at no time is the current flowing, 0 or anywhere near it.

These three classes of currents of course necessitate different types of motors and generators. And the construction of a successful motor involves the application of principles which were not understood for a long time.

The early attempts to operate motors on alternating

currents were naturally far from being successful on this account. The first practical motors wre of the synchronous type, the first one of which was experimented with at North Foreland in 1884. All motors of any account whatever were of this type until the discovery in 1888 of the property of the rotating field as produced by two phase alternating currents. We are indebted to Prof. Ferraris and to Mr. Tesla for the first convincing experiments. These two experimenters reached practically the same conclusion, working independently and simultaneously. Since that time the three phase motor has been developed upon the same lines and the two have been improved mechancially and theoretically until now, as Dr. Bell has pointed out in a recent article, they are equal and in many points superior to the best direct current motors. Dr. Bell believes that they will soon replace to a large extent the old direct current motors in many important industrial applications. ((E. W. XXlV, 124)

Transmission of power by alternating currents we have seen may be accomplished by the use of three different systems.(1) Single Phase, (2) Two Phase and (3) The Three Phase system. The latter two are extremely similar, each having its adherents and opponents. It even seems that most controversies upon the relative merits of the two and three phase currents are, in many respects due to commercial questions rather than engineering details. We will now consider the three methods of transmission or power by alternating currents.

SINGLE PHASE TRANSMISSION.

Single phase currents are practically limited to the transmission of large units of power. In such a case, at the generating station there is an ordinary single phase generator supplying current to step-up transformers perhaps, transmitting power to a motor station where there are step-down transformers to adapt the electro-motive force to the requirements of one synchronous motor. This motor is a machine exactly similar to the generator, being, like it, separately excited. A synchronous motor on a single phase circuit will not start itself, it being necessary to bring it up by some auxiliary apparatus, usually a self-starting motor running on the alternating current or else a direct current motor actuated by storage batteries charged by the exciter.

This non-starting property of synchronous motors is the great cause for their inability to be used in power distribution. However, where it is desired simply to transmit one large unit of power from one locality to a more favorable one the synchronous motor on account of its high efficiency and perfect regulation for varying loads becomes a most valuable machine.

For power distribution in small units the synchronous motor possesses several serious defects other than the one mentioned. Taking all together, the following obstacles present themselves: (1) All synchronous motors must be separately excited, unless a part of the current be communicated; and this would necessitate the addition of a

troublesome commutator to all the other disadvantages. Even then (2) The machine must be started before it will run. It must be turned fast enough to approach the speed of synchronism before the main current is switched on. Of course this is of very small moment when a large plant is to be operated as the additional expense of a small motor would be insignificant; but such a necessary appendage precludes the use of synchronous motors being used by small consumers. Moreover: (3) If the load exceeds a certain amount the motor is thrown out of step and stops immediately, Neither will it start again when the overload is removed: but, unlike a steam engine, waterwheel or any other kind of motor the whole starting process must be repeated. (4) The current lags behind the electro-motive force by an angle which is a maximum at no load and a minimum at full load. Thus under favorable conditions the motor may be returning as much energy to the circuit almost, as is being given to it. Still the same current is flowing and although it may not be doing any usefull work all wires must be made large enough to carry it and the C^2R losses are going on all the time.

(5) All synchronous motors require to be designed not only for given voltage, speed and output, but for a given frequency and therefore can be worked only on given circuits. (6) These motors all have dead points in each p[illegible] thus necessitating their application in such a manner that there will be no danger of stoppage at such points. (7) Synchronous motors can be run at one speed only and that

is the speed which would cause it as a dynamo to generate a current of the same frequency as that supplied it. This of necessity limits its application to those cases where constant speed is either necessary or at least unobjectionable.

There are many other motors adapted to run on single phase currents but few of them are efficient for moderate powers such as would be required in distribution work. There are, it is true, many cases where efficiency does not count for much and it is in such cases that these motors find application. They are mostly, however, of minor importance, being confined to unimportant duties such as driving fans.

Ordinary direct current shunt and series motors have been experimented with, with a view to their application on alternating currents, but with small success. The fields were carefully luminated to prevent loss by Foucault currents. Owing to the difference in the co-efficients of self induction in armature and field of a shunt machine the two currents flowing through each differ in phase thus the periods of minimum and maximum magnetization in each do not coincide, with the result that the motor runs in a very unsatisfactory manner or even may not run at all. The series machine acts somewhat better but it is also very unsatisfactory, the loss by hysteresis is sometimes considerable, the current is made to lag considerably, and the sparking at the brushes is distructive owing to the self induction in the armature coils. In both types the output per unit of weight is very small.

In the shunt type condensers have been resorted to to restore the difference in phase between the two currents but great difficulties have beem encountered. The a action of the condenser is to cause the current tohave a lead over the electro-motive force.

In the first place the condenser must be designed for one given frequency and for a certain angle of advance. Just what angle of advance is necessary is very difficult, one might say impossible, to determine on account of the effects of the armature reactions. Therefore it was found impossible to counteract the effect of self induction. Even could such a thing be done with entirely satisfactory results, the fact still remains that a condenser is a "white elephant" of considerable magnitude. In the first place it is expensive, and in the second place it is liable to get out of order and is susceptible to damaging effects from climate etc. These things will change its capacity and therefore at the same time will cause the angle of advance which it gains to be an unknown quantity.

A more pratical motor than either of these is the induction motor. This depends upon the principle that a closed coil of wire when placed in an alternating field tends to move so that the magnetic flux through it is a minimum. If we take an ordinary armature and place in an alternating magnetic field, short circuiting each coil at the proper time, it will answer the above conditions.

An ordinary two pole motor will, by exciting its field with an alternating current and giving its brushes a forward lead of about 45 degrees fulfill all of these re-

quirements.

Another way of doing it is to place shortcircuited armature coils unsymmetrically with reference to the field. That is, the number of poles in the field and the number of coils in the armature must not have a common factor. A motor built on this plan will not start of its own accord but will rotate in either direction in which it is started. It can however be made self-starting by winding the field coils in two sets of different windings, such that they shall possess different coefficients of self induction; the currents in each therefore differ in phase, and the machine is virtually a two phase motor and self- starting.

The action of this motor is entirely similar to that of the multiphase motors and depends upon the same principle, that of the rotary field. A single phase current may be divided into two branches in which the current may be made to differ in phase by inserting capacity in one branch and self induction in the other. This method, however, leads to the use of the objectionable condenser again. This is virtually an encroachment upon the domain of multiphase currents, and having already alluded to the rotary field and to the self-starting induction motor, it will necessary in order to explain the principles of multi-phase transmission and multiphase motors, that is transmission by either two or three phase currents.

MULTIPHASE TRANSMISSION.

Synchronous motors for multiphase transmission are really synchronous induction motors but unlike single phase synchronous motors they are to a certain extent self-starting. However, what lends additional value to the multiphase system is that all the motors, large and small, are self starting and behave as well as, and often better, than their direct current brethern.

For this we are indebted to the properties possessed by the rotary field several times mentioned. Prof. Ferraris in March 1888 discovered that when two alternating currents, differing in phase from each other by 90 degrees, were passed through two currents placed at right angles to each other they set up a magnetic field which rotated once for every cycle. Now if a closed coil be placed in this magnetic field it will turn so as to keep the magnetic flux through it a minimum as already stated. But since the magnetic field is also moving it follows that the enclosed coil will revolve continually about its axis just as long as the magnetic field rotates.

The coil tries to move so that no currents will be induced in it, in accordance with the well established law which states that a conductor moving in a magnetic field will have a current set up in it in such a direction as to oppose the motion. In the case under consideration it is the magnetic field which moves primarily, thus inducing a current in the conductor which causes the conductor to move so as to stop the current.

Therefore the conductor tries to become stationary with reference to the magnetic field, which it can do only by revolving as fast as the field and in the same direction.

It is plain enough to see why the conductor moves if we grant that the magnetic field rotates as has been said. The reason may be shown simply by means of a figure. We will take the case of two currents which differ 90 degrees in phase. The figure represents an ordinary four pole field with two separate windings.

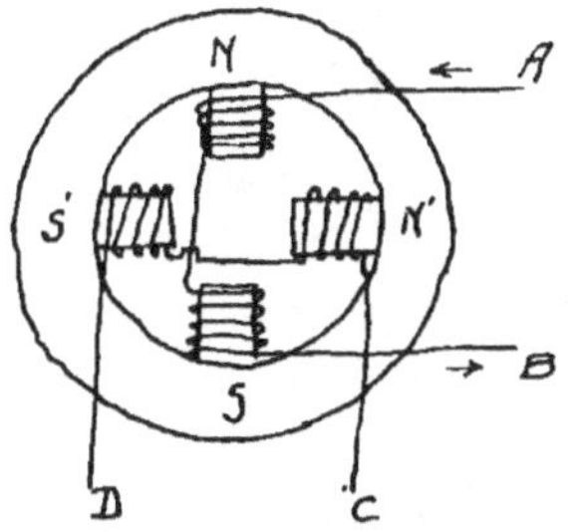

The two windings are placed so that the wires containing one current are wound on opposite poles.

Now since the two currents differ 90 degrees in phase it follows that when one is a maximum the other is a minimum. Suppose current A B is a maximum at the time T, then at that instant there is a north pole at N and a south pole at S, while the other two possess no polarity whatever, but just one quarter of a cycle after, circuit A B is O and C D is a maximum with the resulte that the north pole has shifted to N' and the south pole to S'. And so the action continues, the next quarter cycle finds current A B a maximum but flowing in the reverse direction, so that the north pole is at S and the south pole at N. The final result is then a magnetic field revolving in space about an axis perpindicular to the plane of the diagram. The closed coil in the practical

Therefore the conductor tries to become stationary with reference to the magnetic field, which it can do only by revolving as fast as the field and in the same direction.

It is plain enough to see why the conductor moves if we grant that the magnetic field rotates as has been said. The reason may be shown simply by means of a figure. We will take the case of two currents which differ 90 degrees in phase. The figure repr[illegible] four pole field with two separate windings.

The two [illegible] [illegible] [illegible] [illegible] [illegible] [illegible] [illegible] rents differ [illegible] degrees in phase it follows that when

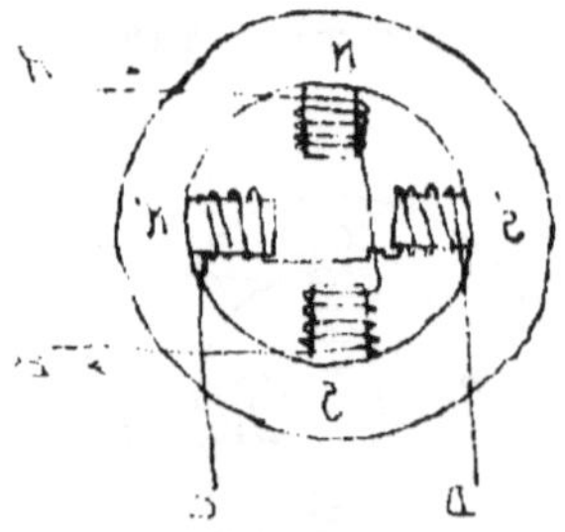

one is a maximum the other is a minimum. Suppose current A B is a maximum at the time T, then at that instant there is a north pole at N and a south pole at S, while the other two possess no polarity whatever, but just one quarter of a cycle after, circuit A B is 0 and C D is a maximum with the result that the north pole has shifted to N' and the south pole to S'. And so the action continues, the next quarter cycle finds current A B a maximum but flowing in the reverse direction, so that the north pole is at S and the south pole at N. The final result is then a magnetic field revolving in space about an axis perpendicular to the plane of the diagram. The closed coil in the practical machine becomes simply a series of closed coils on an armature core, revolving and trying to catch the magnetic poles but never doing so.

The above machine is a rotary field two phase motor and must be supplied by a two phase current. A three phase motor is built on precisely the same principle.

Now in the two phase motor for example, the total magnetizing force in the field at any instant varies from i to 2i sin 45°. (See Fig.)

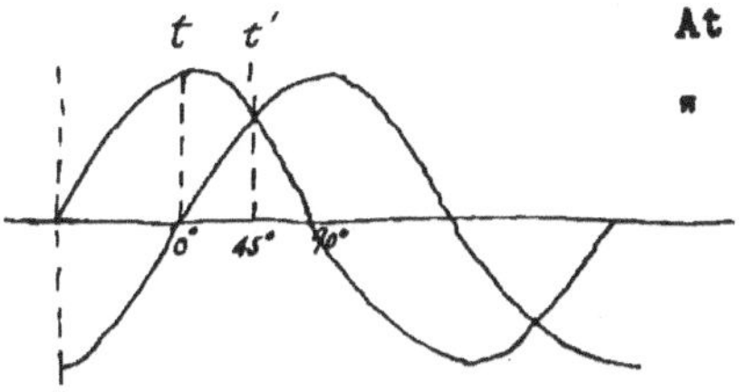

At t sum of currents = i

" t' " " " = i sin 45

+ i sin 45

=2i sin 45

= 1.4 i

Showing that the magnetization varies from a function of i to a function of 1.4 i. This is a variation of 40%, but on account of armature reactions this figure is somewhat modified, it having been shown that the variation is somewhat less than this figure.

Thus it is shown that the motor has not only a rotating field but a pulsating one as well, therefore practice has shown, that, as one would naturally expect from above observations, the motor has a tendency to run synchronously.

Hence it follows that when the motor is not running synchronously the power it is delivering must be the difference between the "positive" power of the rotating field and the "negative" power of the pulsating field. It is "negative power in this case of non-synchronous action on

machine becomes simply a series of closed coils on an armature core, revolving and trying to catch the magnetic poles but never doing so.

The above machine is a rotary field two phase motor and must be supplied by a two phase current. A three phase motor is built on precisely the same principle.

No. in the two phase motor for example, the total magnetizing force in the field at [illegible] varies from 1 to 2 sin 45° (See Fig. [illegible]

Showing that the magnetizing [illegible] varies from [illegible] to a function of 1.4 1. [illegible] a variation of 40%, but on account of armature reactions this figure is somewhat modified, it having been shown that the variation is somewhat less than this figure.

account of the checking influence, which tends to stop the machine. It being a common observation that a synchronous motor stops immediately on getting out of step.

The pulsating character of the field seems to be a great drawback on the face of it, and so it is. It has been found that the two phase motor does not run well on full load, has a marked tendency to synchronism up to certain limits, and beyond those limits speed and torque rapidly decrease. However this motor has the advantage over all motors save the three phase motor that it will start on heavy load.

The three phase motor has a comparatively constant field due to the use of three currents differing 120° in ph phase, so that these objectionable features are almost entirely eliminated. The amount of variation may be shown in the same manner as in the previous case.

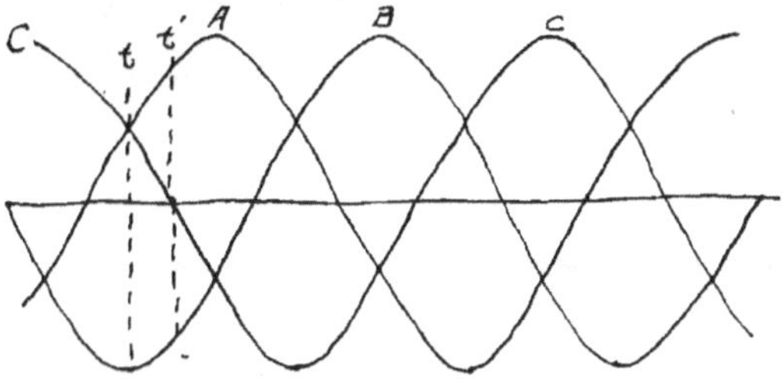

The figure represents three currents differing in phase by 120°

At the time t current A + current C = 2 i sin 30 and B = i.

Therefore since sin 30 = 1/2 it follows that A + B = -B. At the time t, C = 0, A = i sin 60 and B = i sin 120 So C = A +(-B) again. This relation holds good at any time. Therefore at any time any one of the three currents equals minus the sum of the other two.

account of the checking influence, which tends to stop the machine. It being a common observation that a synchronous motor stops immediately on getting out of step.

The pulsating character of the field seems to be a great drawback on the face of it, and so it is. It has been found that the two phase motor does not run well on full load, has a marked tendency to synchronism up to certain limits, and beyond those limits speed and torque rapidly decreases. However this motor has the advantage over all motors save the three phase motor [illegible] on heavy load.

The three phase motor has a [illegible] field due to the use of three currents [illegible] 120 phase, so that these objectionable features [illegible] tirely eliminated. The amount of [illegible] in the same manner as in the previous case.

The figure represents three currents differing in phase by 120

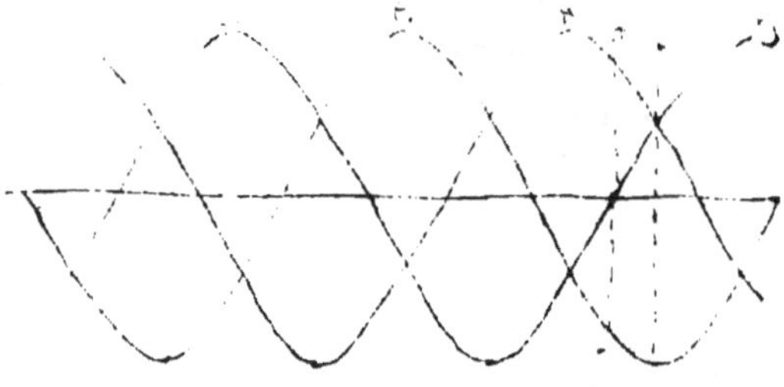

At the time t current A + current C = 2 1 sin 30 and B = 1.

Therefore since sin 30 = 1/2 it follows that A + C = -B. At the time t, C = 0, A = 1 sin 60 and B = 1 sin 120 So C = A +(-B) again. This relation holds good at any time. Therefore at any time any one of the three currents equals minus the sum of the other two.

At t the absolute sum is 2 i and at t' the absolute sum is 1.732i. This is the maximum fluctuation, 2i and 1.732i being the extreme limits. Therefore neglecting armature reactions the magnetization varies (2.00-1.73) ÷ 2. = 14%, as against 40% for the two phase motor. As has already been stated the influence of the armature reactions is to decrease somewhat the range of the pulsations but both motors are effected practically to the same extent. Thus it appears that the two phase field pulsates almost three times more than the three phase field. The effect of this has already been described.

It has been shown that in the case of the three phase current differing 120° in phase the algebraic sum of the three currents is always 0, therefore according to Kirch hoff's law, on current can be connected in series with or in parallel to the other two; this at once suggests a method of winding three phase generator armatures. The windings can be grouped into three series of coils in either of the two following manners.

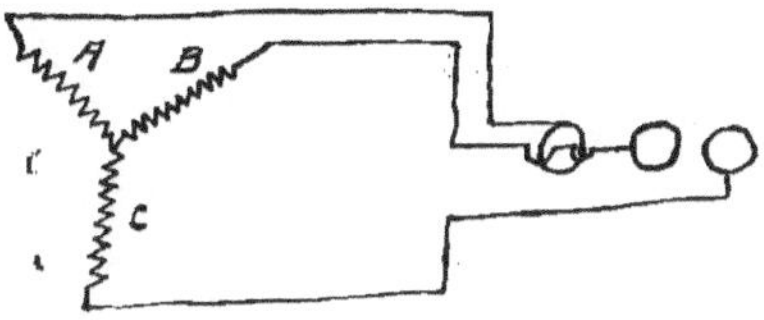

This method is called the open connection, while the other one is known as the closed connection.

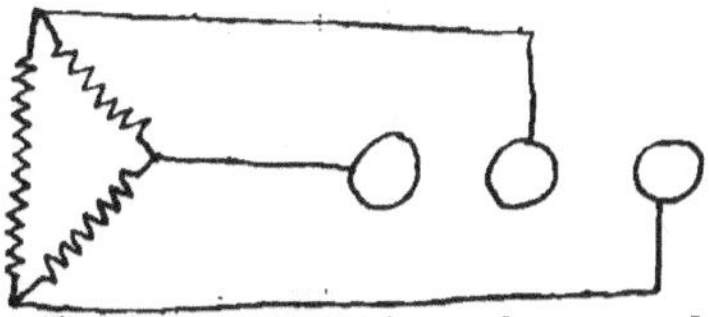

The armature of a Thomson-Houston Arc machine can

At t the absolute sum is 2 t and at t' the absolute sum is 1.7321. This is the maximum fluctuation, 2t and 1.7321 being the extreme limits. Therefore neglecting armature reactions the magnetization varies (2.00-1.73) ÷ 2. = 14%, as against 40% for the two phase motor. As has already been stated the influence of the armature reactions is to decrease somewhat the range of the pulsations but both motors are effected practically to the same extent. Thus it appears that the two phase field pulsates almost three times more than the three phase field. The effect of this has already been described.

It has been shown that in the case of the three phase current differing 120° in phase the algebraic sum of the three currents is always 0, therefore according to Kirchhoff's law, on current can be connected in series with or in parallel to the other two; this at once suggests a method of winding three phase generator armatures. The windings can be grouped into three series of coils in either of the two following manners.

This method is called the open connection,

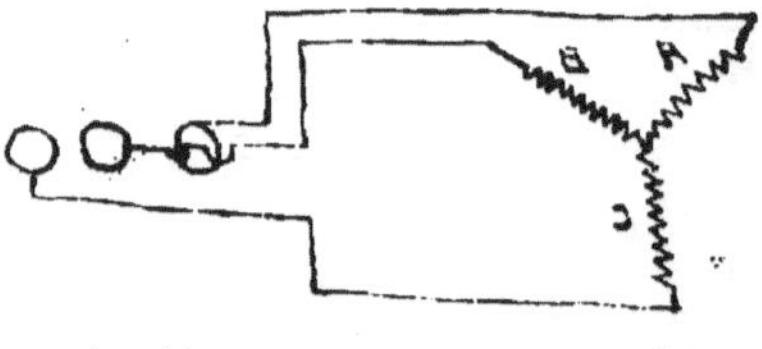

while the other one is known as the closed connection.

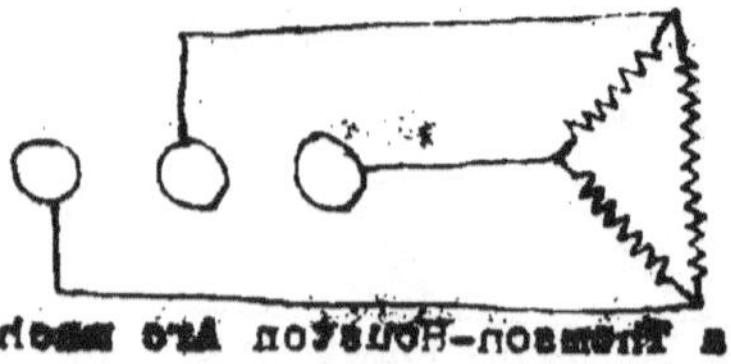

The armature of a Thomson-Houston Arc machine can

by the addition of three collecting rings be made into a three phase armature. In the same manner any armature may be altered to give three phase currents with but little trouble.

Rotary field motors are extremely simple, there being no sliding contacts, and the armature being wound with heavy bars of copper connected across the ends, making a good mechanical structure, far excelling direct current armatures in point of durability and freedon from liability to heat.

Dabrowalsky made careful and exhaustive tests with a three phase motor and found it absolutely devoid of synchronous action, and when compared with a good direct current motor os similar output, actually showed higher efficience. He also found that they gave greatér output for the same weight than ordinary motors, and this despite the lag produced in the exciting current and the "magnetic slip"

When the current lags behind the electro-motive force the power in it expressed in watts is:

$$E' I' \cos \phi$$

where ϕ is the angle of lag. Cos ϕ is what is called the <u>power factor</u>, the maximum value of which is 1. This corfesponds to an angle of 0° for cos $0 = 1$. Hence it becomes evident that the greater the power factor becomes the smaller the useless idle current becomes. That is we do not have to use large wire for a large current when only a small part of it is useful.

The maximum value of the power factor being unity, the cosine of the angle of lag expresses when multiplied

by 10, percent directly. The power factor is therefore generally spoken of as so much per cent. As the load increases the lag decreases so that the power factor increases, a very good characteristic. Rotary field motors are now built with power factors as high as 90%.

<u>Magnetic slip</u>. It has been shown that the armature of a rotary field tends to rotate fast enough to catch the magnetic field. As a matter of fact it never does. There is always a difference in the frequency of the dynamo. This difference is the "magnetic slip".

Polyphase motors have a tendency to run in phase with the generator and when they are in step ~~with~~ the magnetic slip is 0.

Calling frequency of generator = ng

and " " motor = nm

The slip becomes ng- nm, and the per cent of slip is:

(ng- nm) ÷ ng.

The frequency and the magnitude of the armature current evidently depends upon the magnetic slip, for the rate of cutting of the lines of force in the field depends upon the difference between the speed of the field and the speed of the armature.

Slip increases both the frequency and the current in the armature, thereby weakening the resultant magnetic field and the counter electro-motive-force of the field winding, allowing more current to flow through it.

The total magnetization decreases as the armature

by 10, percent directly. The power factor is therefore generally spoken of as so much per cent. As the load increases the lag decreases so that the power factor increases, a very good characteristic. Rotary field motors are now built with power factors as high as 90%.

Magnetic slip. It has been shown that the armature of a rotary field tends to rotate fast enough to catch the magnetic field. As a matter of fact it never does. There is always a difference in the frequency of [illegible] dynamo. This difference is the "magnetic slip".

Polyphase motors have a tendency to [illegible] with the generator and when they are in step [illegible] netic slip is 0.

Calling frequency of generator = ng

and " " motor nm

The slip becomes ng- nm, and the per cent of slip is:

(ng- nm) ÷ ng.

The frequency and the magnitude of the armature current evidently depends upon the magnetic slip, for the rate of cutting of the lines of force in the field depends upon the difference between the speed of the field and the speed of the armature.

Slip increases both the frequency and the current in the armature, thereby weakening the resultant magnetic field and the counter [illegible] of the field windings, allowing more current to flow through it.

The total magnetization decreases as the armature

current increases there is therefore some condition of affairs during which the torque is a maximum, this condition is evidently not the one where the armature current is a m maximum, that is when the machine is starting. Therefore we see it is impossible for these motors to exert their maximum torque on starting.

MONOCYCLIC SYSTEM.

Within the last few months there has been introduced a new (?) system of power distribution called by the inventors "Monocyclic System" The generator is wound like an ordinary single phase machine with the exception that a supplementary winding or "teaser" coil, connected in the middle of the main winding and the terminal brought to the third collecting ring. From this third collecting ring a wire is run to those points, and those points only, where power is needed. This system it is claimed possesses all of the advantages of a single phase system with regard to facility of regulation, with the additional advantage that it is able to carry polyphase motor loads.

This third winding is so proportioned that the resultant e. m. f. is composed of the electro-motive-forces differing 60° in phase.

Now if in the apparatus for transformation one of these e. m. f.s is reversed we have three currents differing in phase by 120°. However, it is claimed that this supplemental coil as ordinarily used has no effect upon the voltage of the two outside wires, so that they may be used for lighting in the ordinary way. But when it is desired to run a motor two transformers are inserted between the power wire and each of the two other ones, with the secondary of one reversed so as to give three currents 120° apart. In this circuit may be inserted an ordinary three phase motor.

W Where the subsidary e. m. f. is generated is of small moment, power may be generated by single phase generators and at the point where a motor is required the displaced e. m. f. may be generated by a synchronous motor, thus doing away with the third wire for great distances.

The motors are designed so as to cause a counter e. m. f. in the power wire of such magnitude that no current flows in it, so that it may be disconnected entirely.

The chief advantage of this system appears to be in central station distribution where a great many lights as well as motors are required.

It would seem from what has been said that for transmission of power through long distances three phase currents are best particularly as they only require 75% as much wire as the single phase phase and the two complete circuit two phase system. The three phase system however is rather difficult to handle in lighting, so for distribution involving lighting and power the two phase and monocyclic systems are superior.

By means of transformers with suitably proportioned windings it is practicable to convert from two phase and vice versa. Consequently a judicious admixture of the two systems would seem to offer an ideal solution of the problem.

The copper used by each system is easily calculated. Dr. Bell has secured the following results. Taking single phase system as the base:

Single phase two wire-	Copper	100.0

Two Phase	4 wire	Copper	100.0
Three "	3 "	"	75.0
Two "	3	"(using same voltage	145.5
Three "	4	2	29.2
Monocyclic as ordinarily used			100-125.

The three phase system is therefore the most economical of wire for all of the practical systems.

With regard to the frequency of alternating currents we find in machines as now made quite a large range. In as much as the old standard of single phase system was 133 some companies manufacture motors still to run on that frequency. Now, however, the tendency is to lower this.

Impedance depends upon frequency $=\sqrt{R^2+(2\pi n^2L)^2}$ where n is the frequency. Thus we see that it is desirable to have the frequency as low as possible to make the impedance of the motors small. When the impedance is great the angle of lag between e. m. f. and current is great, causing a large idle current to flow in the motor fields. In other words the power factor is made small.

But there is a limit to the lowness of the frequency and that is the minimum at which electric lights will burn steadily. This minimum is about 35; below this lamps flicker noticeably. The usual practic now is to adopt a frequency of about 60, this being applicable to both power and light. In plants where the transmission of power is the prime factor and lighting is a minor consideration, n is often as low as 25.

In order to carry on some experiments in alternating currents of different numbers of phases and different frequencies a 15 horse power multipolar Crocker-Wheeler motor was so connected as to give three phase alternating currents. This result was accomplished by connecting the commutator parts of the ordinary armature to three connecting rings in such a way that the three currents were taken off as alternating currents . After a little experimentation it was clearly demonstrated that the curves of the electromotive- force of these three phase alternating currents were very far from true sinusoidal curves. Subsequently some experiments were tried upon a Thomson-Houston open coil arc machine, three connecting rings having been placed just outside the three bar commutator. Finding this on the whole unsatisfactory it was decided to [redacted]ct an "Experimental Generator", the idea being to so arrange the winding on the armature that it could be used as a 500 volt constant potential generator or motor also.

In the case of the dynamo we added the series turns effect to the shunt turns and in the case of the motor would be so connected that the ampere turns in series would tend to counteract the ampere turns of the shunt winding.

In making the armature it was decided to use a toothed core and in winding the connections were so left that any of the following combinations could be used.

1. A constant potential continuous current dynamo.
2. A constant potential continuous motor.
3. A single phase constant potential alternating current

dynamo having frequency of 40, which it was possible to increase and having an electro-motive force of 1000 volts.

4. A two phase alternating current dynamo of 250 volts difference of potential.

5. A three phase alternating dynamo of 133 volts difference of potential.

The details of the armature are shown in the blue prints. The reason for making a machine of this character was that it was possible to combine in one machine a generator which could be used for a large number of different purposes and it is believed that it will be a valuable adjunct to our electrical laboratory here. The machine is now in course of construction and will be completed within a very short time. The design of this machine will now be given. By reference to the blue prints the general dimensions and characteristic feature of the generator will be easily sean.

ASSUMPTIONS.

The dynamo is designed to give 40 amperes at a potential of 500 volts at the brushes. The peripheral velocity is to be rather high, 3600 ft per sec., because the machine is to be rather small for its output in volts. The design is to resemble a 15 horse power Crocker-Wheeler motor.

r% will be assumed as 72.2%, this is that of the C-W machine, any two poles covering 130° on the armature. The armature will have a toothed core practically the same size as the C-W motor. That is 12" diameter and 8" long. The thickness of the ring will be 3".

For high speed, multipolar, toothed ring armature of 20 K. W. capacity an allowance of 5400 lines of force per [illegible]/cm. in the field is good practice (A. E. Wiener, Electrical World)

COMPUTATIONS.

$\frac{\text{Total current}}{4} = \frac{40}{4} =$ 10 amperes = current in each conductor, since armature is divided into four parallel circuits.

Size of Armature Conductor

Allow 500 circular mils per ampere, will require wire of cross section of

5000 circular mils = #13 B&S (5179)

Diam bare #13 = 0.072

Insulation = 0.02

ASSUMPTIONS.

The dynamo is designed to give 40 amperes at a potential of 500 volts at the brushes. The peripheral velocity is to be rather high, 3600 ft per sec., because the machine is to be rather small for its output in volts. The design is to resemble a 15 horse power Crocker-Wheeler motor.

ϕ will be assumed as 72.2%, this is % of the C-W machine, say two poles covering 130 on armature. The armature will have a toothed core practically the same size as the C-W motor. That is 12" diameter and " long. The thickness of the ring will be 3".

For high speed, multipolar, toothed ring armature of 20 K. W. capacity an allowance of 5400 lines of force per sq. cm. in the field is good practice (A. E. Wiener, Electrical World)

COMPUTATIONS.

$\frac{\text{Total current}}{4} = \frac{40}{4} =$ 10 amperes = current in each conductor, since armature is divided into four parallel circuits.

Size of Armature Conductor

Allow 500 circular mils per ampere, will require wire of cross section of

5000 circular mils = #13 B&S (5179)

Diam bare #13 = 0.072

Insulation =0.02

Total Diameter = 0."092

Length of actice wire

Volts per cm active wire =

$$\frac{B_{g} \text{ X Peripheral vel. X } 30.5 \text{ X } \pi\%}{10^8 \text{ X } 60}$$

$$= \frac{5400 \text{ X } 3600 \text{ X } 30.5 \text{ X } .722}{10^8 \text{ X } 60}$$

= .083 (volts per cm active wire

$$\frac{500 \text{ X } 4}{.083} = 24096 \text{ cm wire for 500 volts}$$

$$\frac{24096}{30.5} = 790 \text{ feet active wire.}$$

Dimensions of teeth and slots.

It has been determined by practice that a toothed armature with rectangular slots and trapezoidal teeth the width of a slot should be that of the top of a tooth. To get the proper number of teeth the allowable difference in potential between adjacent commutator bars must be considered.

In a machine of this type and of similar output practice has shown that a difference of potential of 20 volts may be allowed.

In this machine between bars 90° apart the difference of potential is 500 volts, therefore $\frac{500}{20}$ = 25 gives number of bars in 1/4 of armature = 100 bars for the whole = 100 teeth = 100 slots.

12" X π = 37".49 circum. of Armature.

width slot

$$\frac{37".49}{2 \text{ X } 100} = 0".187 \text{ width of slot}$$

= 3/16"

and 0".184 = diameter 2 # 13 wires.

Can therefore wind two 2 No. 13 wires side by side.

$\frac{790}{100} = 7'.9 = 94'.8$ necessary length of wire in each slot.

$\frac{94.8}{8 \text{ (l of arm.)}} = 11+$ say 12 wires in every slot. This gives then 2 wires wide and 6 deep

0.092 width of 1 # 12

6

Depth slot — $.552 = 9/16$ depth of slot

Check for l. of active wire

$$l = \frac{8^{\text{[l of arm]}} \times 12^{\text{[no. conductors]}} \times 100^{\text{[no. slots]}}}{12} = 800 \text{ feet}$$

Calculated = 790'

Actual = 800'

From large drawing width of tooth at bottom was found to be 11/16" being only 1/64" less than top.

Armature will be "bar wound" every conductor will be connected with another 90° away.

Ratio total to active — Then from drawing to scale $\frac{\text{Total wire}}{\text{Active}} = \frac{3}{1}$

Resistance of Armature

$$R = \frac{10.8\ L'}{\text{Cir. Mils}}$$

$$= \frac{10.8 \times 3 \times 800}{5180} \times \frac{1}{16} \text{ (Four\# circuits)}$$

$= 0.311$ ohms

Drop in Potential — Drop in potential = C R

= 40 X .311

= 12.4 volts

and 0.184" = diameter 2 # 13 wires.

Can therefore wind two 2 No. 13 wires side by side.

$\frac{790}{100} = 7.9 \times 12 = 94.8$ necessary length of wire in each slot.

$\frac{94.8}{8}$ (l of arm.) = 11+ say 12 wires in every slot. This gives then 2 wires wide and 6 deep

0.092 width of 1" 12

Depth slot $\frac{6}{.552}$ = 9/16 depth of slot

Check for l. of active wire

$l = \frac{8 \text{ (l. arm)} \times 12 \times 100}{12} = 800$ feet

Calculated = 790'

Actual = 800'

From large drawing width of tooth at bottom was found to be 11/16" being only 1/64" less than top.

Armature will be "bar wound" every conductor will be connected with another 90° away.

Ratio total to active

Then from drawing to scale $\frac{\text{Total wire}}{\text{Active}} = \frac{3}{1}$

Resistance of Armature

$R = \frac{10.8 \, L}{\text{Cir. Mils}}$

$= \frac{10.8 \times 3 \times 800}{6530} \times \frac{1}{16}$ (Four circuits)

= 0.311 ohms

Drop in

Drop in potential = C R

= 40 X .311 =

Heat loss   Loss = E = C^2R = 12.4 X 40

= 497.6 watts

% loss $\frac{497}{20000}$ = 2.48% loss

Magnetic Circuit

Air space   By drawing to scale, allowing 1/16" for clearance, 1/32" for binding wires and somewhat over 1/2 (5/9) of length of tooth for space taken up by conductors, A_g = 0".42 = 1.07 cm for one pole

$$si = \frac{Hl}{1.26}$$

$$= \frac{5400 \times 2.14}{1.26}$$

Amp. turns for Air space   = 9172 amp. turns for Air space

From the same drawing.

Length of Iron Circ.   L. of mag. circuit is in wrt Fe 52 cm

" " " " " " cast Fe 36 cm

Allowing v = 1.4 i.e. 40% leakage

B_{core} = $\frac{5400}{.60}$ = 9000 =

For B = 9000 in Wrt Fe H = 4

$$si = \frac{Hl}{1.26}$$

$$= \frac{52 \times 4}{1.26}$$

Amp. turns for Wrt Fe   = 165 amp. turns for wrt iron

Between each wrt iron core there is a cast iron yoke 5" X 8".5 through which 1/2 of B_{core} goes

1/2 area core = $\frac{\pi d^2}{2 \times 4}$ = $5.5^2 \pi$

= 12.6 Sq. inches.

Area yoke = 3 X 8.5 = 25.5 Sq. In.

Hence $\frac{B_{core}}{B_{yoke}} = \frac{25.5}{12.5} = \frac{2}{1}$

Then B in cast iron will be 4500

For B = 4500 in. cast iron H = 7.5

And $si = \frac{Hl}{1.26}$

Ampere turns for Cast Fe

$= \frac{7.5 \times 56}{1.26}$

= 340 Ampere turns cast Fe

Then total ampere turns on field will be:

9172 for air space

165 wrt iron circuit

340 for cast iron circuit

9677 total.

Size of Wire

It is now necessary to determine the size of wire on the field

Circular mils $= \frac{10.8 \; si \times l' \text{ of average turn}}{125}$

In this formula 125 represents 1/4 of the total voltage as the four field coils are in series.

Wire may be easily wound to the depth of 3 1/2 inches

Hence diameter average turn is:

9" length is 28.27 = 2.35

Then:

Circular mils $= \frac{10.8 \times 9677 \times 2.35}{125}$

Allowing 1000 circular mils per ampere this
will carry 2 amperes.

Then no. turns on each core is:

Turns on Cores

$$\frac{9677}{2} = 4832$$

Diam bare #17 = 0".045

Insulation = 0".02

Total 0.065

No. layers etc.

$$\frac{3.5}{.065} = 53.8 = 54 \text{ No. layers of wire}$$

$$\frac{4832}{54} = 89.5 = 90 = \text{No. wires in layer}$$

0.065 X 90 = 5.8 length of core winding.

Series Coil

The compounding coil will be wound outside of this in a space 6" long. It must carry
40 amperes. Allowing 10000 circular mils per ampere will
require 40000 circular mils = #4(41743)

Diam. bare #4 = 0".20

Insulation = 0".02

Total Diam. 0".22

$$\frac{6}{.22} = 27 \text{ turns. This will give 1080 ampere}$$
turns to compensate for drop in potential in
armature.

Losses.

(1) Armature

(a) $C_a^2 R_a$ = 497.6 watts (page 3-4)

(b) Hysteresis

Watts lost = $\dfrac{H_a I \times \text{vol. cu. cm} \times c \times c \text{ per sec.}}{10^7}$

Hysteresis

Vol. of armature.

Mean depth ring = 3", mean diam. 9", length = 8'

allowing 1000 circular mils per ampere this will carry 2 amperes.

Then no. turns on each core is:

Turns on Cores

$\frac{9677}{2} = 4838$

Diam bare #17 = 0.045

Insulation = 0.02

Total 0.065

No. layers etc.

$\frac{3.5}{.065} = 53.8 = 54$ No. layers of wire

$\frac{4838}{54} = 89.5 = 90 =$ No. turns [illegible]

0.065 X 90 = 5.85 length of core [illegible]

Series Coil

The compounding coils will [illegible] side of this in a space 6" long.

40 amperes. Allowing 1000 circular mils [illegible] require 40000 circular mils = [illegible]

Diam. bare #4 = 0.20

Insulation = 0.02

Total Diam. 0.22

$\frac{6}{.22} =$ 27 turns. This will give 1080 ampere turns to compensate for drop in potential in armature.

Losses.

(1) Armature

(a) C^2R_a = 497.6 watts (page 3-4)

(b) Hysteresis

Hysteresis

Watts loss = $\frac{\eta B^{1.6} \times \text{vol. cu. cm} \times \text{cyc per sec.}}{10^7}$

Vol. of armature.

Mean depth rings 3", mean diam. 9", length = 9"

Vol. = $3 \times 7 \times \pi \times 9 = 678.48$ [redacted]

This neglects the ~~pressure~~ volume of the slots, so is too large; but the increased hysteresis in the teeth has also been neglected

Hysteresis

$678.48 \times 2.54^3 = 11127$ Cu. c.

But 90 % of this is iron on account of the lamination, paper etc.

$11127 \times .9 = 10014$

Induction in armature

Hysteresis

$$\frac{B_a}{B_f} = \frac{A_{field}}{A_{armature}} = \frac{\frac{1/2\,\pi\,(\text{diam. pole})^2}{4}}{24} = \frac{12.6}{24}$$

= practically 1 to 2 $\therefore B_a = 4500$

$$\text{Cycles per sec.} = \frac{\text{Rev per min.}}{60} \times \frac{4}{2}$$

$$= \frac{1200}{60} \times 2 = 40$$

For $B = 4500$, $\int H\,dI = 1465$

Hence Watts lost =

$$\frac{1465 \times 10000 \times 40}{10^7} = 58.6$$ [redacted]

Foucault Currents

(c) Foucault Currents

W lost $= x^2 \times B^2 \times n^2 \times 10^{-16} \times$ vol.

where x = thickness of disc in mils = 50

n = cycles per sec [redacted] = 40

$$\text{Watts lost} = \frac{2500 \times 20250000 \times 10000 \times 1600}{10^{16}}$$

= 81 watts

Friction

(d) Friction = 2% output = $20000 \times .02$

= 400 watts

(2) Field Loss

(2) Field Loss.

Field loss (a) Shunt coil loss is E C = 500 X 2= 1000 watts

(b) Series coil L' of turn $= \frac{\pi \times 12.75}{12} = 3'.2$

Loss in

Series 3.2 X 27 X 4= total ℓ series coil in ft = 345'.6

Coil R of 345'.6 = .086 ohm

Then C^2R= 1600 X .086 = 137.6 watts

COMMERCIAL EFFICIENCY

Useful output = 38 amperes at 487.6 volts

Total looses are:

C_a^2R = 497.6 watts

Hysteresis= 58.6 "

Foucault Cur. 81.0 "

Friction 400.0 "

Shunt Field1000.0 "

Series " 137.6

2174.8 "

Efficiency = [redacted] / 38 X 487.6 + 2174.8

Efficiency

= 89.5%

www.ingramcontent.com/pod-product-compliance
Lightning Source LLC
Chambersburg PA
CBHW021517090426
42739CB00007B/663
* 9 7 8 3 3 3 7 1 9 2 4 3 3 *